ALUMINUM CROCHET HOOKS

UNITED STATES	METRIC (mm)
B-1	2.25
C-2	2.75
D-3	3.25
E-4	3.50
F-5	3.75
G-6	4.00
H-8	5.00
I-9	5.50
J-10	6.00
K-10½	6.50
N	9.00
P	10.00
Q	15.00

GAUGE

Exact gauge is **essential** for proper size. Hook size given in instructions is merely a guide and should never be used without first making a sample swatch of the rows or rounds indicated in the yarn and hook specified. Then measure the swatch, counting your stitches and rows or rounds carefully. If your swatch is larger or smaller than specified, **make another, changing hook size to get the correct gauge**. Keep trying until you find the size hook that will give you the specified gauge.

JOINING WITH SC

When instructed to join with sc, begin with a slip knot on hook. Insert hook in stitch indicated, YO and pull up a loop, YO and draw through both loops on hook.

BACK RIDGE

Work only in loop(s) indicated by arrows *(Fig. 1)*.

Fig. 1

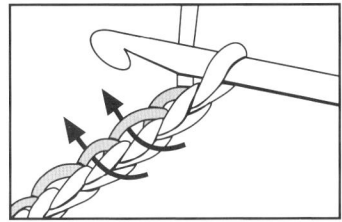

BACK LOOP ONLY

Work only in loop(s) indicated by arrow *(Fig. 2)*.

Fig. 2

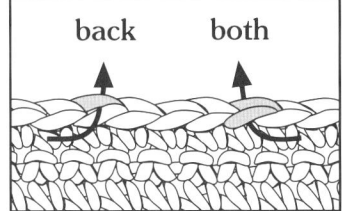

FREE LOOPS OF A CHAIN

When instructed to work in free loops of a chain, work in loop indicated by arrow *(Fig. 3)*.

Fig. 3

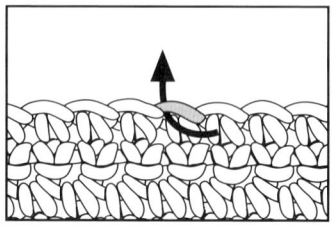

WORKING INTO A CHAIN

When instructed to work under top 2 loops of a chain, work under loops indicated by arrow *(Fig. 4)*.

Fig. 4

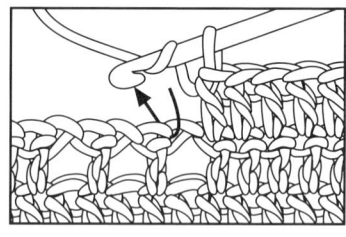

WHIPSTITCH

Place two pieces with **wrong** sides together. Beginning in second ch of first corner ch-2, sew through both pieces once to secure the beginning of the seam, leaving an ample yarn end to weave in later. Working through **both** loops of each stitch of **both** pieces, insert the needle from front to back through first stitch and pull yarn through *(Fig. 5)*, ★ insert the needle from front to back through next stitch and pull yarn through; repeat from ★ across to first ch of next corner ch-2.

Fig. 5

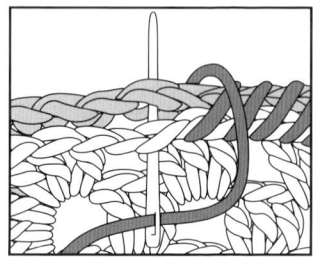

FRINGE

Cut a piece of cardboard about 5" wide and half as long as length specified in instructions. Wind the yarn **loosely** and **evenly** around the cardboard lengthwise until the card is filled, then cut across one end; repeat as needed.

Hold together as many strands of yarn as specified in individual instructions; fold in half.

With **wrong** side facing and using a crochet hook, draw the folded end up through a row, stitch, or space and pull the loose ends through the folded end *(Fig. 6a or 6c)*; draw the knot up **tightly** *(Fig. 6b or 6d)*. Lay flat on a hard surface and trim the ends.

Fig. 6a

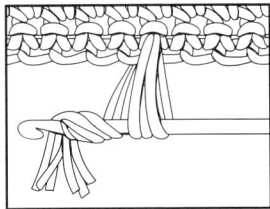

Fig. 6b

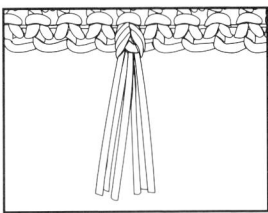

Fig. 6c

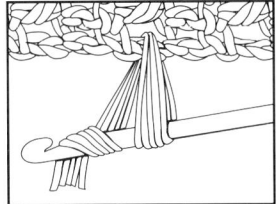

Fig. 6d

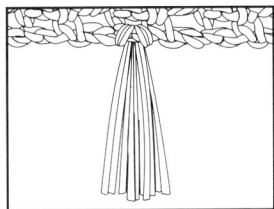

1. RAINBOW SQUARES
Shown on page 9.

Finished Size:
31" x 39"

MATERIALS
Sport Weight Yarn:
White - 20 ounces,
(570 grams, 1,885 yards)
Purple - 1 ounce,
(30 grams, 95 yards)
Blue - 1 ounce,
(30 grams, 95 yards)
Green - 1 ounce,
(30 grams, 95 yards)
Yellow - 1 ounce,
(30 grams, 95 yards)
Peach - 1 ounce,
(30 grams, 95 yards)
Pink - 1 ounce,
(30 grams, 95 yards)
Crochet hook, size J (6.00 mm) **or** size needed for gauge
Yarn needle

Note: Afghan is worked holding two strands of yarn together.

GAUGE SWATCH: 8" square
Work same as Block A.

BLOCK A (Make 6)
Holding one strand of White and one strand of Purple together, ch 3; join with slip st to form a ring.

To work Puff St (uses one st or sp), ★ YO, insert hook in st or sp indicated, YO and pull up a loop even with loop on hook; repeat from ★ once **more**, YO and draw through all 5 loops on hook.

4

Rnd 1 (Right side)**:** Pull up a 1/2" loop, (work Puff St in ring, ch 1) 8 times; join with slip st to top of first Puff St, finish off: 8 ch-1 sps.

Note: Loop a short piece of yarn around any stitch to mark Rnd 1 as **right** side.

To work extended single crochet (abbreviated *ex sc*), insert hook in st or sp indicated, YO and pull up a loop, YO and draw through one loop on hook, YO and draw through both loops on hook.

Rnd 2: With **right** side facing and holding one strand of White and one strand of Blue together, join yarn with slip st in any ch-1 sp; pull up a 1/2" loop, work (Puff St, ch 2, Puff St) in same sp, ch 1, ex sc in next ch-1 sp, ch 1, ★ work (Puff St, ch 2, Puff St) in next ch-1 sp, ch 1, ex sc in next ch-1 sp, ch 1; repeat from ★ 2 times **more**; join with slip st to top of first Puff St, finish off: 12 sts and 12 sps.

Rnd 3: With **right** side facing and holding one strand of White and one strand of Green together, join yarn with slip st in any corner ch-2 sp; pull up a 1/2" loop, work (Puff St, ch 2, Puff St) in same sp, ch 1, ex sc in next ch-1 sp, ex sc in next ex sc and in next ch-1 sp, ch 1, ★ work (Puff St, ch 2, Puff St) in next corner ch-2 sp, ch 1, ex sc in next ch-1 sp, ex sc in next ex sc and in next ch-1 sp, ch 1; repeat from ★ 2 times **more**; join with slip st to top of first Puff St, finish off: 12 ex sc.

Rnd 4: With **right** side facing and holding one strand of White and one strand of Yellow together, join yarn with slip st in any corner ch-2 sp; pull up a 1/2" loop, work (Puff St, ch 2, Puff St) in same sp, ch 1, ex sc in each ch-1 sp and in each ex sc across to next corner ch-2 sp, ch 1, ★ work (Puff St, ch 2, Puff St) in corner ch-2 sp, ch 1, ex sc in each ch-1 sp and in each ex sc across to next corner ch-2 sp, ch 1; repeat from ★ 2 times **more**; join with slip st to top of first Puff St, finish off: 20 ex sc.

Rnd 5: Holding one strand of White and one strand of Peach together, repeat Rnd 4: 28 ex sc.

Rnd 6: Holding one strand of White and one strand of Pink together, repeat Rnd 4: 36 ex sc.

Rnd 7: With **right** side facing and holding two strands of White together, join yarn with slip st in any corner ch-2 sp; pull up a 1/2" loop, work (Puff St, ch 2, Puff St) in same sp, ch 1, ex sc in each ch-1 sp and in Back Loop Only *(Fig. 2, page 2)* of each ex sc across to next corner ch-2 sp, ch 1, ★ work (Puff St, ch 2, Puff St) in corner ch-2 sp, ch 1, ex sc in each ch-1 sp and in Back Loop Only of each ex sc across to next corner ch-2 sp, ch 1; repeat from ★ 2 times **more**; join with slip st to top of first Puff St: 44 ex sc.

Rnds 8-10: Slip st in first corner ch-2 sp, pull up a $1/2$" loop, work (Puff St, ch 2, Puff St) in same sp, ch 1, ex sc in each ch-1 sp and in both loops of each ex sc across to next corner ch-2 sp, ch 1, ★ work (Puff St, ch 2, Puff St) in corner ch-2 sp, ch 1, ex sc in each ch-1 sp and in both loops of each ex sc across to next corner ch-2 sp, ch 1; repeat from ★ 2 times **more**; join with slip st to top of first Puff St: 68 ex sc.

Finish off.

BLOCK B (Make 6)

Holding one strand of White and one strand of Pink together, ch 3; join with slip st to form a ring.

Rnd 1 (Right side)**:** Pull up a $1/2$" loop, (work Puff St in ring, ch 1) 8 times; join with slip st to top of first Puff St, finish off: 8 ch-1 sps.

Note: Mark Rnd 1 as **right** side.

Rnd 2: With **right** side facing and holding one strand of White and one strand of Peach together, join yarn with slip st in any ch-1 sp; pull up a $1/2$" loop, work (Puff St, ch 2, Puff St) in same sp, ch 1, ex sc in next ch-1 sp, ch 1, ★ work (Puff St, ch 2, Puff St) in next ch-1 sp, ch 1, ex sc in next ch-1 sp, ch 1; repeat from ★ 2 times **more**; join with slip st to top of first Puff St, finish off: 12 sts and 12 sps.

Rnd 3: With **right** side facing and holding one strand of White and one strand of Yellow together, join yarn with slip st in any corner ch-2 sp; pull up a $1/2$" loop, work (Puff St, ch 2, Puff St) in same sp, ch 1, ex sc in next ch-1 sp, ex sc in next ex sc and in next ch-1 sp, ch 1, ★ work (Puff St, ch 2, Puff St) in next corner ch-2 sp, ch 1, ex sc in next ch-1 sp, ex sc in next ex sc and in next ch-1 sp, ch 1; repeat from ★ 2 times **more**; join with slip st to top of first Puff St, finish off: 12 ex sc.

Rnd 4: With **right** side facing and holding one strand of White and one strand of Green together, join yarn with slip st in any corner ch-2 sp; pull up a $1/2$" loop, work (Puff St, ch 2, Puff St) in same sp, ch 1, ex sc in each ch-1 sp and in each ex sc across to next corner ch-2 sp, ch 1, ★ work (Puff St, ch 2, Puff St) in corner ch-2 sp, ch 1, ex sc in each ch-1 sp and in each ex sc across to next corner ch-2 sp, ch 1; repeat from ★ 2 times **more**; join with slip st to top of first Puff St, finish off: 20 ex sc.

Rnd 5: Holding one strand of White and one strand of Blue together, repeat Rnd 4: 28 ex sc.

Rnd 6: Holding one strand of White and one strand of Purple together, repeat Rnd 4: 36 ex sc.

Rnds 7-10: Work same as Block A: 68 ex sc.

Finish off.

ASSEMBLY

Holding two strands of White together and using Placement Diagram as a guide, whipstitch Blocks together forming 3 vertical strips of 4 Blocks each *(Fig. 5, page 3)*; then whipstitch strips together in same manner.

PLACEMENT DIAGRAM

A	B	A
B	A	B
A	B	A
B	A	B

BORDER

To decrease (uses next 2 ch-2 sps), ★ YO, insert hook in **next** ch-2 sp, YO and pull up a loop even with loop on hook, YO, insert hook in **same** sp, YO and pull up a loop even with loop on hook; repeat from ★ once **more**, YO and draw through all 9 loops on hook.

Rnd 1: With **right** side of one long edge facing and holding two strands of White together, join yarn with slip st in top right corner ch-2 sp; pull up a $1/2$" loop, work (Puff St, ch 2, Puff St) in same sp, ★ † ex sc in next ch-1 sp and in each ex sc across to next ch-1 sp, ex sc in ch-1 sp, (decrease, ex sc in next ch-1 sp and in each ex sc across to next ch-1 sp, ex sc in ch-1 sp) across to next corner ch-2 sp †, work (Puff St, ch 2, Puff St) in corner ch-2 sp; repeat from ★ 2 times **more**, then repeat from † to † once; join with slip st to top of first Puff St: 284 sts and 4 ch-2 sps.

Rnd 2: Slip st in first ch-2 sp, pull up a $1/2$" loop, work (Puff St, ch 2, Puff St) in same sp, † ch 1, skip next 3 sts, (work Puff St, ch 1) twice in next ex sc, [skip next 2 sts, (work Puff St, ch 1) twice in next ex sc] 6 times, ★ skip next ex sc, (work Puff St, ch 1) twice in next ex sc, [skip next 2 sts, (work Puff St, ch 1) twice in next ex sc] 6 times; repeat from ★ once **more**, skip next ex sc, (work Puff St, ch 1) twice in next ex sc, skip next 2 ex sc, [(work Puff St, ch 1) twice in next ex sc, skip next 2 sts] 5 times, work (Puff St, ch 2, Puff St) in next ch-2 sp, ch 1, skip next 3 sts, (work Puff St, ch 1) twice in next ex sc, [skip next 2 sts, (work Puff St, ch 1) twice in next ex sc] 6 times, skip next ex sc, (work Puff St, ch 1) twice in next ex sc, [skip next 2 sts, (work Puff St, ch 1) twice in next ex sc] 6 times, skip next ex sc, (work Puff St, ch 1) twice in next ex sc, skip next 2 ex sc, [(work Puff St, ch 1) twice in next ex sc, skip next 2 sts] 5 times †, work (Puff St, ch 2, Puff St) in next ch-2 sp, repeat from † to † once; join with slip st to top of first Puff St: 192 ch-1 sps and 4 ch-2 sps.

Rnd 3: Slip st in first ch-2 sp, pull up a 1/2" loop, work (Puff St, ch 2, Puff St) in same sp, ch 1, ★ † work Puff St in next ch-1 sp, ch 1, (work Puff St, ch 1) twice in next ch-1 sp, [skip next ch-1 sp, (work Puff St, ch 1) twice in next ch-1 sp] across to within one ch-1 sp of next corner ch-2 sp, work Puff St in ch-1 sp, ch 1 †, work (Puff St, ch 2, Puff St) in corner ch-2 sp, ch 1; repeat from ★ 2 times **more**, then repeat from † to † once; join with slip st to top of first Puff St: 200 ch-1 sps and 4 ch-2 sps.

Rnd 4: Slip st in first ch-2 sp, ch 2, (ex sc, ch 1, 2 ex sc) in same sp, † ex sc in next 2 ch-1 sps, 2 ex sc in next ch-1 sp, (ex sc in next ch-1 sp, 2 ex sc in next ch-1 sp) across to next corner ch-2 sp, (2 ex sc, ch 1, 2 ex sc) in corner ch-2 sp, 2 ex sc in next ch-1 sp, (ex sc in next ch-1 sp, 2 ex sc in next ch-1 sp) across to next corner ch-2 sp †, (2 ex sc, ch 1, 2 ex sc) in corner ch-2 sp, repeat from † to † once; join with slip st to top of beginning ch-2: 316 sts and 4 ch-1 sps.

Rnds 5-8: Slip st in first ch-1 sp, ch 3, ex sc in same sp and in each ex sc across to next corner ch-1 sp, ★ (ex sc, ch 1, ex sc) in corner ch-1 sp, ex sc in each ex sc across to next corner ch-1 sp; repeat from ★ 2 times **more**; join with slip st to second ch of beginning ch-3: 348 sts and 4 ch-1 sps.

Rnd 9: Slip st in first ch-1 sp, pull up a 1/2" loop, work Puff St in same sp, (ch 2, work Puff St in same sp) twice, ch 1, ★ † slip st in next ex sc, ch 1, [skip next ex sc, (work Puff St, ch 1) twice in next ex sc, skip next ex sc, slip st in next ex sc, ch 1] across to next corner ch-1 sp †, work Puff St in corner ch-1 sp, (ch 2, work Puff St in same sp) twice, ch 1; repeat from ★ 2 times **more**, then repeat from † to † once; join with slip st to top of first Puff St, finish off.

Design by C. A. Riley.

2. BLUE MEDLEY

Shown on Front Cover.

Finished Size:
36" x 45 1/2"

MATERIALS
Worsted Weight Yarn:
Variegated - 19 ounces,
(540 grams, 1,075 yards)
Blue - 19 ounces,
(540 grams, 1,075 yards)
Crochet hook, size P (10.00 mm) **or** size needed for gauge

Note: Each row is worked across length of Afghan holding two strands of yarn together.

GAUGE: In pattern,
2 repeats = $2^3/_4$"; 4 rows = 3"

Gauge Swatch: $4^1/_2$"w x 4"h
Holding one strand of Variegated and one strand of Blue together, ch 12 **loosely**. Work same as Afghan for 5 rows.
Finish off.

AFGHAN
Holding one strand of Variegated and one strand of Blue together, ch 102 **loosely**.

Row 1 (Right side)**:** Dc in back ridge of fourth ch from hook *(Fig. 1, page 2)* and each ch across **(3 skipped chs count as first dc)**: 100 dc.

Note: Loop a short piece of yarn around any stitch to mark Row 1 as **right** side.

Row 2: Ch 1, turn; sc in first dc, ★ ch 2, skip next 2 dc, sc in next dc; repeat from ★ across: 34 sc and 33 ch-2 sps.

Row 3: Ch 3 **(counts as first dc, now and throughout)**, turn; (2 dc in next ch-2 sp, dc in next sc) across: 100 dc.

Row 4: Ch 1, turn; sc in first dc, ★ ch 2, skip next 2 dc, sc in next dc; repeat from ★ across: 34 sc and 33 ch-2 sps.

Row 5: Ch 3, turn; (2 dc in next ch-2 sp, dc in next sc) across: 100 dc.

Repeat Rows 4 and 5 until Afghan measures approximately 36" from beginning ch, ending by working Row 5.

Finish off.

Holding 4 strands of Variegated and 4 strands of Blue together, each 16" long, add fringe in end of each right side row across short edges of Afghan *(Figs. 6c & d, page 4)*.

Design by Carole Prior.

3. PASTEL STRIPES
Shown on Back Cover.

Finished Size:
34" x 46¹/₂"

MATERIALS
Sport Weight Yarn:
White - 21 ounces,
(600 grams, 1,680 yards)
Green - 6 ounces,
(170 grams, 480 yards)
Pink - 6 ounces,
(170 grams, 480 yards)
Blue - 6 ounces,
(170 grams, 480 yards)
Yellow - 4$^{1}/_{2}$ ounces,
(130 grams, 360 yards)
Crochet hook, size J (6.00 mm) **or** size needed for gauge

Note: Each row is worked across length of Afghan holding two strands of yarn together. When joining yarn and finishing off, leave a 7" end to be worked into fringe.

GAUGE: In pattern,
12 sts and 8 rows = 4"

Gauge Swatch: 6$^{1}/_{4}$"w x 4"h
Holding two strands of White together, ch 21 **loosely**.
Work same as Afghan for 8 rows.

AFGHAN BODY
Holding two strands of White together, ch 141 **loosely**.

Row 1 (Right side)**:** Dc in fourth ch from hook **(3 skipped chs count as first dc)** and in each ch across; finish off: 139 dc.

Note: Loop a short piece of yarn around any stitch to mark Row 1 as **right** side.

To work Cluster (uses one dc), ★ YO, insert hook in dc indicated, YO and pull up a loop, YO and draw through 2 loops on hook; repeat from ★ 2 times **more**, YO and draw through all 4 loops on hook.

Row 2: With **wrong** side facing and holding two strands of Green together, join yarn with sc in first dc *(see Joining With Sc, page 2)*; sc in next 2 dc, (work Cluster in next dc, sc in next 3 dc) across; finish off: 34 Clusters and 105 sc.

Row 3: With **right** side facing and holding one strand of Green and one strand of White together, join yarn with slip st in first sc; ch 3 **(counts as first dc, now and throughout)**, dc in next 4 sts, ch 1, ★ skip next sc, dc in next 7 sts, ch 1; repeat from ★ across to last 6 sts, skip next sc, dc in last 5 sts; finish off: 122 dc and 17 chs.

Row 4: With **wrong** side facing and holding one strand of Green and one strand of White together, join yarn with slip st in first dc; ch 3, dc in next 2 dc, ★ ch 1, skip next dc, (dc in next dc, ch 1) twice, skip next dc, dc in next 3 dc; repeat from ★ across; finish off: 88 dc and 51 chs.

Note: When working into a chain, insert hook under top 2 loops *(Fig. 4, page 3)*.

Row 5: With **right** side facing and holding one strand of Green and one strand of White together, join yarn with slip st in first dc; ch 3, dc in next 2 dc, ★ dc in next ch and in next dc, ch 1, skip next ch, dc in next dc and in next ch, dc in next 3 dc; repeat from ★ across; finish off: 122 dc and 17 chs.

Row 6: With **wrong** side facing and holding two strands of Green together, join yarn with sc in first dc; sc in next 2 dc, ★ work Cluster in next dc, sc in next dc, sc in next ch and in next dc, work Cluster in next dc, sc in next 3 dc; repeat from ★ across; finish off: 34 Clusters and 105 sc.

Row 7: With **right** side facing and holding two strands of White together, join yarn with slip st in first sc; ch 3, dc in next sc and in each st across; finish off: 139 dc.

Row 8: With **wrong** side facing and holding two strands of Pink together, join yarn with sc in first dc; sc in next 2 dc, (work Cluster in next dc, sc in next 3 dc) across; finish off: 34 Clusters and 105 sc.

Row 9: With **right** side facing and holding one strand of Pink and one strand of White together, join yarn with slip st in first sc; ch 3, dc in next 4 sts, ch 1, ★ skip next sc, dc in next 7 sts, ch 1; repeat from ★ across to last 6 sts, skip next sc, dc in last 5 sts; finish off: 122 dc and 17 chs.

Row 10: With **wrong** side facing and holding one strand of Pink and one strand of White together, join yarn with slip st in first dc; ch 3, dc in next 2 dc, ★ ch 1, skip next dc, (dc in next dc, ch 1) twice, skip next dc, dc in next 3 dc; repeat from ★ across; finish off: 88 dc and 51 chs.

Row 11: With **right** side facing and holding one strand of Pink and one strand of White together, join yarn with slip st in first dc; ch 3, dc in next 2 dc, ★ dc in next ch and in next dc, ch 1, skip next ch, dc in next dc and in next ch, dc in next 3 dc; repeat from ★ across; finish off: 122 dc and 17 chs.

Row 12: Holding two strands of Pink together, repeat Row 6.

Row 13: Repeat Row 7.

Row 14: Holding two strands of Blue together, repeat Row 8.

Rows 15-17: Holding one strand of Blue and one strand of White together, repeat Rows 9-11.

Row 18: Holding two strands of Blue together, repeat Row 6.

Row 19: Repeat Row 7.

Row 20: Holding two strands of Yellow together, repeat Row 8.

Rows 21-23: Holding one strand of Yellow and one strand of White together, repeat Rows 9-11.

Row 24: Holding two strands of Yellow together, repeat Row 6.

Row 25: Repeat Row 7.

Row 26: Holding two strands of Green together, repeat Row 8.

Rows 27-29: Holding one strand of Green and one strand of White together, repeat Rows 9-11.

Rows 30-67: Repeat Rows 6-29 once, then repeat Rows 6-19 once **more**.

EDGING
FIRST SIDE
Row 1: With **wrong** side facing and holding two strands of White together, join yarn with sc in first dc on Row 67; sc in next dc, ch 1, ★ skip next dc, sc in next dc, ch 1; repeat from ★ across to last 3 dc, skip next dc, sc in last 2 dc: 71 sc and 68 ch-1 sps.

Row 2: Ch 1, turn; slip st in first sc, ch 1, (slip st in next ch-1 sp, ch 1) across to last 2 sc, skip next sc, slip st in last sc; finish off.

SECOND SIDE
Row 1: With **wrong** side facing, holding two strands of White together and working in free loops of beginning ch *(Fig. 3, page 3)*, join yarn with sc in ch at base of first dc; sc in next ch, ch 1, ★ skip next ch, sc in next ch, ch 1; repeat from ★ across to last 3 chs, skip next ch, sc in last 2 chs: 71 sc and 68 ch-1 sps.

Row 2: Ch 1, turn; slip st in first sc, ch 1, (slip st in next ch-1 sp, ch 1) across to last 2 sc, skip next sc, slip st in last sc; finish off.

Holding desired number of strands together, each 14" long, add additional fringe in end of wrong side rows *(Figs. 6c & d, page 4)*.

Design by Anne Halliday.

4. RAINBOW RIPPLE

Shown on Back Cover.

Finished Size:
33" x 45"

MATERIALS
Sport Weight Yarn:
Blue - 8 ounces,
(230 grams, 640 yards)
White - 6^1/$_2$ ounces,
(180 grams, 520 yards)
Green - 5^1/$_2$ ounces,
(160 grams, 440 yards)
Yellow - 5^1/$_2$ ounces,
(160 grams, 440 yards)
Pink - 5^1/$_2$ ounces,
(160 grams, 440 yards)
Crochet hook, size J (6.00 mm) **or** size needed for gauge

Note: Afghan is worked holding two strands of yarn together.

GAUGE: In pattern,
from point to point = 4";
8 rows = 4^3/$_4$"

Gauge Swatch:
8^1/$_2$"w x 4^3/$_4$"h
Holding two strands of Blue together, ch 33 **loosely**.
Work same as Afghan for 8 rows.
Finish off.

AFGHAN BODY

Holding two strands of Blue together, ch 129 **loosely**.

Row 1 (Wrong side)**:** Sc in second ch from hook and in next 7 chs, ch 2, ★ sc in next 7 chs, skip next 2 chs, sc in next 7 chs, ch 2; repeat from ★ across to last 8 chs, sc in last 8 chs: 114 sc and 8 ch-2 sps.

Note: Loop a short piece of yarn around **back** of any stitch on Row 1 to mark **right** side.

To decrease (uses next 4 sc), YO, insert hook in next sc, YO and pull up a loop, YO and draw through 2 loops on hook, YO, skip next 2 sc, insert hook in next sc, YO and pull up a loop, YO and draw through 2 loops on hook, YO and draw through all 3 loops on hook **(counts as one dc)**.

To work ending decrease (uses last 3 sc), YO, insert hook in next sc, YO and pull up a loop, YO and draw through 2 loops on hook, YO, skip next sc, insert hook in last sc, YO and pull up a loop, YO and draw through 2 loops on hook, YO and draw through all 3 loops on hook **(counts as one dc)**.

Row 2: Ch 2, turn; skip first 2 sc, dc in next 6 sc, (dc, ch 2, dc) in next ch-2 sp, ch 1, (skip next sc, dc in next sc, ch 1) twice,

★ skip next sc, decrease, dc in next 5 sc, (dc, ch 2, dc) in next ch-2 sp, ch 1, (skip next sc, dc in next sc, ch 1) twice; repeat from ★ across to last 4 sc, skip next sc, work ending decrease: 81 dc and 32 sps.

Note: When working into a chain, insert hook under top 2 loops *(Fig. 4, page 3)*.

Row 3: Ch 1, turn; sc in first dc, (sc in next ch and in next dc) 3 times, (sc, ch 2, sc) in next ch-2 sp, ★ sc in next 6 dc, skip next dc, (sc in next ch and in next dc) 3 times, (sc, ch 2, sc) in next ch-2 sp; repeat from ★ across to last 7 dc, sc in last 7 dc; finish off: 114 sc and 8 ch-2 sps.

To work beginning decrease (uses first 3 sc), ch 2, YO, skip next sc, insert hook in next sc, YO and pull up a loop, (YO and draw through 2 loops on hook) twice **(counts as one dc)**.

Row 4: With **right** side facing and holding two strands of Green together, join yarn with slip st in first sc; work beginning decrease, dc in next 5 sc, (dc, ch 2, dc) in next ch-2 sp, ch 1, (skip next sc, dc in next sc, ch 1) twice, ★ skip next sc, decrease, dc in next 5 sc, (dc, ch 2, dc) in next ch-2 sp, ch 1, (skip next sc, dc in next sc, ch 1) twice; repeat from ★ across to last 4 sc, skip next sc, work ending decrease: 81 dc and 32 sps.

Row 5: Ch 1, turn; sc in first dc, (sc in next ch and in next dc) 3 times, (sc, ch 2, sc) in next ch-2 sp, ★ sc in next 6 dc, skip next dc, (sc in next ch and in next dc) 3 times, (sc, ch 2, sc) in next ch-2 sp; repeat from ★ across to last 7 dc, sc in last 7 dc; finish off: 114 sc and 8 ch-2 sps.

Rows 6 and 7: Holding two strands of Yellow together, repeat Rows 4 and 5.

Rows 8 and 9: Holding two strands of Pink together, repeat Rows 4 and 5.

Rows 10 and 11: Holding one strand of Blue and one strand of White together, repeat Rows 4 and 5.

Rows 12 and 13: Holding one strand of Green and one strand of White together, repeat Rows 4 and 5.

Rows 14 and 15: Holding one strand of Yellow and one strand of White together, repeat Rows 4 and 5.

Rows 16 and 17: Holding one strand of Pink and one strand of White together, repeat Rows 4 and 5.

Rows 18 and 19: Holding two strands of Blue together, repeat Rows 4 and 5.

Rows 20-73: Repeat Rows 4-19, 3 times; then repeat Rows 4-9 once **more**.

Row 74: With **right** side facing and holding two strands of Blue together, join yarn with slip st in first sc; work beginning decrease, dc in next 5 sc, (dc, ch 2, dc) in next ch-2 sp, ch 1, (skip next sc, dc in next sc, ch 1) twice, ★ skip next sc, decrease, dc in next 5 sc, (dc, ch 2, dc) in next ch-2 sp, ch 1, (skip next sc, dc in next sc, ch 1) twice; repeat from ★ across to last 4 sc, skip next sc, work ending decrease: 81 dc and 32 sps.

Row 75: Ch 1, turn; sc in first dc, (sc in next ch and in next dc) 3 times, (sc, ch 2, sc) in next ch-2 sp, ★ sc in next 6 dc, skip next dc, (sc in next ch and in next dc) 3 times, (sc, ch 2, sc) in next ch-2 sp; repeat from ★ across to last 7 dc, sc in last 7 dc; do **not** finish off: 114 sc and 8 ch-2 sps.

EDGING

To work Cluster, ch 3, dc in third ch from hook.

Ch 1, turn; slip st in first sc, ch 2, skip next sc, (slip st in next sc, ch 2, skip next sc) 3 times, (slip st, ch 2) twice in next ch-2 sp, [skip next sc, (slip st in next sc, ch 2, skip next sc) twice, slip st in next 4 sc, ch 2, skip next sc, (slip st in next sc, ch 2, skip next sc) twice, (slip st, ch 2) twice in next ch-2 sp] across to last 8 sc, skip next sc, slip st in next sc, (ch 2, skip next sc, slip st in next sc) 3 times, work Cluster; working in end of rows, skip first 2 rows, slip st in next row, work Cluster, (skip next row, slip st in next row, work Cluster) across; working in free loops *(Fig. 3, page 3)* and in sps across beginning ch, slip st in ch at base of first sc, ch 2, skip next ch, (slip st in next ch, ch 2, skip next ch) twice, slip st in next 4 chs, [ch 2, skip next ch, (slip st in next ch, ch 2, skip next ch) twice, (slip st, ch 2) twice in next sp, skip next ch, (slip st in next ch, ch 2, skip next ch) twice, slip st in next 4 chs] across to last 6 chs, (ch 2, skip next ch, slip st in next ch) 3 times, work Cluster; working in end of rows, slip st in first row, work Cluster, (skip next row, slip st in next row, work Cluster) across to last 2 rows, skip last 2 rows; join with slip st to first slip st, finish off.

Design by Anne Halliday.